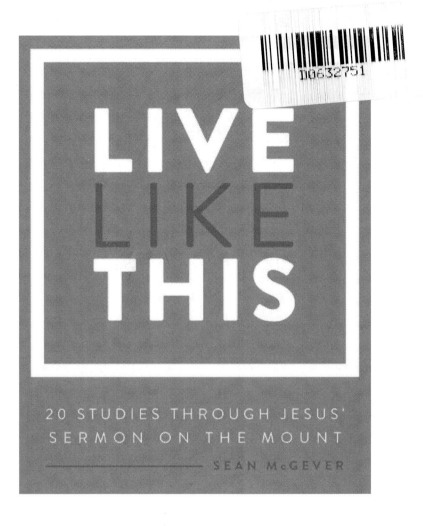

LIVE LIKE THIS

20 STUDIES THROUGH JESUS' SERMON ON THE MOUNT

SEAN McGEVER

Cover designed by fisherdesign.co.uk

Live Like This Copyright © 2010, 2017, 3rd ed. All rights reserved.

CALIMO, Sean McGever, seanmcgever.com, smcgever@gmail.com

ISBN: 1975675479
ISBN-13: 978-1975675479

Live Like This is inspired by the incredible discussions I've had with my Young Life friends over many years. Live Like This can be used in a small group or on your own. Another way to use it is to have people in your group complete it on their own and then meet up as a group to share your answers.

If you get together with some friends, here are several tips I highly recommend as part of your time:

- Have food or snacks (seriously!)
- Share about your past week. My friends call it "High/Low," the high point of your last week and the low point of the last week. Some call it "Happy/Crappy," but you can call it whatever you want.
- Read the Scriptures out of your own Bible. The verses are provided for your convenience, but it is best to become familiar with your own Bible.
- The "Live Like This" section at the end of each study provides a place to summarize in one word what you have learned, want to remember, and/or apply to your life.
- Pray at the end of your time.

I hope this helps you!

Sean McGever

Special thanks to my Wiffleball Wednesday guys from Pinnacle High School who spent a year studying the Sermon on the Mount together. We learned to hit the curve ball and more about Jesus.

I would like to thank the writing of John R. W. Stott. Many helpful resources were used in the research for this booklet, but none were more insightful then Stott's "The Message of the Sermon on the Mount" in the Bible Speaks Today Commentary Series by Inter-Varsity Press. Stott sub-titled his book "Christian Counter-Culture" and I feel the kingdom of God shines more brightly because of his insights. I pray I can lovingly embrace our culture while living counter to it.

Sean McGever is an Area Director for Young Life in Phoenix, Arizona. He has spent nearly a decade posting club plans, leadership ideas, games, skits, talk ideas, and much more at YLHelp.com. His primary focus is to make the most of his unique capacity as an experienced YL leader and staff person combined with his formal theological training as a theologian and professor of theology.

Intro to "Live Like This" and the Sermon on the Mount

In your hands, you hold what many consider to be the most famous teachings the world has ever seen on how to live an incredible life. Jesus said a lot of things, but for many people, the most challenging and inspiring things Jesus said are in the "Sermon on the Mount."

The Sermon on the Mount is the longest recorded speech we have from Jesus. This sermon came early in the ministry of Jesus. Jesus was baptized, spent 40 days in the desert, chose a small group of followers, and then gave this sermon. We can think of the Sermon on the Mount as Jesus' initial training, Jesus' primary message, and the first things that Jesus wanted everyone to know about how to live a God-honoring life.

You will see that the Sermon on the Mount is incredibly practical – covering topics such as anger, prayer, worry, money and more. This booklet goes through each topic one by one. The subjects are incredibly diverse. At one point you will be reading about keeping your word, soon after you will be reading about fasting. One nice thing about reading through the Bible is that you allow the Bible to set the agenda. In effect, you are letting Jesus choose the topics. The topics covered in the Sermon on the Mount are:

1. Attitude	11. Prayer (part 2)
2. Obedience	12. Forgiveness
3. Bible	13. Fasting
4. Anger	14. Heart
5. Lust	15. Worry
6. Integrity	16. Judging
7. Retaliation	17. Prayer (part 3)
8. Love	18. Loneliness
9. Giving	19. Fruitfulness
10. Prayer (part 1)	20. Review

One recurring theme in the Sermon on the Mount is being "counter-culture" for Jesus Christ. Those who choose to "Live Like This" will have very different lifestyles than the rest of the world. People will wonder why you live your life the way you do. In fact, your life will speak for itself. "Let your good deeds shine out for all to see, so that everyone will praise your heavenly Father." (Matthew 5:16)

Contents

1: Attitude

Matthew 5:1-12

¹One day as he saw the crowds gathering, Jesus went up on the mountainside and sat down. His disciples gathered around him, ²and he began to teach them. ³"God blesses those who are poor and realize their need for him, for the Kingdom of Heaven is theirs. ⁴God blesses those who mourn, for they will be comforted. ⁵God blesses those who are humble, for they will inherit the whole earth. ⁶God blesses those who hunger and thirst for justice, for they will be satisfied. ⁷God blesses those who are merciful, for they will be shown mercy. ⁸God blesses those whose hearts are pure, for they will see God. ⁹God blesses those who work for peace, for they will be called the children of God. ¹⁰God blesses those who are persecuted for doing right, for the Kingdom of Heaven is theirs. ¹¹"God blesses you when people mock you and persecute you and lie about you and say all sorts of evil things against you because you are my followers. ¹²Be happy about it! Be very glad! For a great reward awaits you in heaven. And remember, the ancient prophets were persecuted in the same way.

Some of the best conversations are created when friends sit around and talk about life. This is how Jesus begins the Sermon on the Mount. There were crowds gathered (see the beginning of verse 1); but, at first, Jesus focuses on His closest friends, the disciples (see the end of verse 1).

In the first ten verses, Jesus says "God blesses…" eight different times. These are traditionally called the "beatitudes." One easy way to think of them is the "be attitudes," or the attitudes of a person in a relationship with Jesus Christ; or in other words, one who calls themselves a Christian.

In times like ours, the word "blessed" can mean a lot of things. The word Jesus used is meant to communicate something similar to our modern meaning of "blessed," but slightly different. "Happy," "fortunate," or "well off," might be more what Jesus was saying. Substituting these words changes our understanding. Instead of "Blessed are those who mourn," we could say "Happy/fortunate/well-off are those who mourn". How can you be happy when you mourn? This is exactly what Jesus wants us to think about.

Jesus ends this section by talking about a great reward that awaits those who live for him. Learning to live for Jesus will be the hardest thing you ever do, but living for Jesus will also be more rewarding then you could ever imagine!

1. What friends would you pick to sit around and have a deep conversation with about the most important things in life?

2. How is it possible to be blessed/fortunate/well-off when difficult or challenging things happen in your life? Share an example.

Blessed / Happy are those who are	→	For
Poor and realize their need for God	→	The Kingdom of heaven is theirs
Mourn	→	They will be comforted
Humble	→	They will inherit the whole earth
Hunger and thirst for justice	→	They will be satisfied
Merciful	→	They will be shown mercy
Heart is pure	→	They will see God
Work for peace	→	They will be called children of God
Persecuted for doing right	→	The Kingdom of heaven is theirs

3. Which one of the descriptions above have you experienced in your life? What did you learn from it?

4. Which one of the outcomes (the "For" column) would you *like* to experience? How can you experience this in your life?

5. Which one of the attitudes in these verses do you feel like you need in your life now?

Live Like This:
One word that sums it up for you

2: Obedience

¹³"You are the salt of the earth. But what good is salt if it has lost its flavor? Can you make it salty again? It will be thrown out and trampled underfoot as worthless. ¹⁴"You are the light of the world—like a city on a hilltop that cannot be hidden. ¹⁵No one lights a lamp and then puts it under a basket. Instead, a lamp is placed on a stand, where it gives light to everyone in the house. ¹⁶In the same way, let your good deeds shine out for all to see, so that everyone will praise your heavenly Father.

Let's be very clear here. Jesus is speaking to those who call themselves Christians – Jesus says "you ARE the salt of the earth." The real question is whether those who call themselves Christians are doing their job. The goal is that "everyone will praise your heavenly Father" (5:13). Christians are supposed to be recognized by their good deeds. Jesus uses two everyday illustrations to help communicate how this is possible.

Everyone knows what salt tastes like. If you think about salt for a moment, you can probably start salivating in your mouth right now! Salt helps bring out the flavor in food. Not only that, but salt is also used as a preservative, especially when refrigeration isn't available. In other words, salt can prevent decay; salt can keep things from wasting away. Christians are called to help life be sustained, to be kept fresh. Christians are called to keep life from being wasted away. Because of this, a Christian should not blend into the culture and the ways of the world. A Christian must find ways for their life to not be wasted away.

Close your eyes. Wherever you are, at this very second, you are experiencing the benefits of light. Your experience of life would be very different without light. Imagine staring at the Grand Canyon in absolute darkness. Christians are called to illuminate the world. That means to bring out and highlight what life is all about: truth, love, joy, peace, patience, kindness, and abundant life, just to name a few things. Christians are to be visibly different *in order to* attract attention to God.

What Jesus is saying is that *how* a Christian lives is very important. If your deeds and actions are the same as a person who isn't a Christian, then your example is what Jesus says in verse 13, it is "worthless." [Note: "You" aren't worthless, your *example* is worthless. You are inherently and unendingly valuable since God created you in His image, see Genesis 1:27.] There should be a noticeable difference in a Christian. We are called to accept our role as "salt" and "light" to the people we know.

1. What kind of spices do you like to add to certain foods? Why does it taste better?

2. What do you think people notice about your personality and day-to-day actions?

3. Who lights up your world? Why?

4. Suppose that everyone who is not a Christian lived in the dark all the time. How could a person who is a Christian help illuminate their life?

5. Do you know anyone (without naming names) who claims to be a Christian, but their actions look just like everyone else's? How does that make you feel? How do you think Jesus feels about that?

6. Why do you think Christians might be tempted to "hide their light"?

7. Who is an example of a person you know who has been "salt" and "light" in your life? How have they done that?

Live Like This:
One word that sums it up for you

3: Bible

Matthew 5:17-20

[17]*"Don't misunderstand why I have come. I did not come to abolish the law of Moses or the writings of the prophets. No, I came to accomplish their purpose.* [18]*I tell you the truth, until heaven and earth disappear, not even the smallest detail of God's law will disappear until its purpose is achieved.* [19]*So if you ignore the least commandment and teach others to do the same, you will be called the least in the Kingdom of Heaven. But anyone who obeys God's laws and teaches them will be called great in the Kingdom of Heaven.* [20]*"But I warn you—unless your righteousness is better than the righteousness of the teachers of religious law and the Pharisees, you will never enter the Kingdom of Heaven!"*

The Bible has two main parts: the Old Testament and the New Testament. The Old Testament covers history and teaching from the beginning of time until about 400BC. The New Testament covers history and teaching from the birth of Jesus (0AD) until about 70AD.

The Old Testament includes three main parts: Law, History and Prophets. The Law is a collection of instructions from God. The History books contain the history of the Jewish people. The Prophets are a collection of teaching and predictive words, or prophecy, about how the Jewish people should respond right then and God's plans for the future.

The Law portion of the Old Testament contains 248 commandments and 365 prohibitions, or things that are forbidden. In Jesus' day, there was a group of people called the Pharisees. The Pharisees tried very hard to obey everything in the Old Testament and felt like they had to remind people often about each of these rules.

When Jesus says, "unless your righteousness is better than the righteousness of... Pharisees," Jesus does not intend for us to get a better "score" then the Pharisees. No one needs to think, "I obeyed 200 out of 248 today, how about you?" What Jesus is saying is that Jesus' life accomplished our right-standing with God. What Jesus is also saying is "external obedience" is not the key to life, but what is inside is what counts. Jesus wants us to genuinely obey because we *want to* rather than because we *have to*. A verse in the Old Testament puts it this way, "People judge by outward appearance, but the Lord looks at the heart." (1 Samuel 16:7)

If we truly want to be great, then we must learn what the Bible has to say about life and desire to see it change us from the inside out.

1. What is a topic you know a lot about?

2. What would be more convincing to you: a person telling an important personal story from his or her life or an actor telling that same story? Why? What does this say about being "genuine"?

3. Have you ever been taught about the Bible or read it yourself? If so, describe what this has been like.

4. Which part of the Bible sounds most interesting to you? Why?
> *Old Testament Law*: Instructions from God.
> *Old Testament History*: History of Jewish people.
> *Old Testament Prophets*: Prophecy about the future.
> *New Testament*: Life of Jesus and further teaching.

5. Would you like to learn more about the Bible? If not, why? If yes, how would you do that?

6. What is something from the Bible that you genuinely want to obey in your life?

Live Like This:
One word that sums it up for you

4: Anger

21 *"You have heard that our ancestors were told, 'You must not murder. If you commit murder, you are subject to judgment.'* 22 *But I say, if you are even angry with someone, you are subject to judgment! If you call someone an idiot, you are in danger of being brought before the court. And if you curse someone, you are in danger of the fires of hell.* 23 *"So if you are presenting a sacrifice at the altar in the Temple and you suddenly remember that someone has something against you,* 24 *leave your sacrifice there at the altar. Go and be reconciled to that person. Then come and offer your sacrifice to God.* 25 *"When you are on the way to court with your adversary, settle your differences quickly. Otherwise, your accuser may hand you over to the judge, who will hand you over to an officer, and you will be thrown into prison.* 26 *And if that happens, you surely won't be free again until you have paid the last penny.*

Do you get angry? We all do! God knew we would all struggle with anger. In fact, over 3000 years ago, when the Ten Commandments were written, the ultimate expression of anger was included: "Do not murder" (Deuteronomy 20:13). In Matthew 5:21-26, Jesus shares some practical and spiritual advice about anger.

In verse 22, Jesus says that anger has the same outcome as murder. The root of murder includes an element of anger. Not all anger is bad. God can be angry with a "righteous anger." Jesus was clearly angry for the right reason when He cleared the temple of the greedy salespeople (John 2:13-16). Yet, our anger is rarely righteous and pure like Jesus'.

One way we express anger is name-calling. Calling someone an "idiot," or cursing them, which means calling them a "fool" or "stupid," comes with some heavy consequences. There is nothing magical about the specific words. What is more important is the meaning that is behind the words, the angry attitude that causes angry words.

So what are we supposed to do when we get angry? First, don't let it come out in thoughtless words. Next, as it says in verses 23-26, go immediately to the person, without waiting, and "be reconciled" or "make peace" with them. Jesus will give more direction on this in Matthew 7:1-5. One suggestion is to look at your own faults before you attack someone else's. When you are angry, ask God in prayer to help you with your thoughts, body language (rolling your eyes, turning away, etc.), and words.

1. Describe a time when someone was really angry with you.

2. Describe a time when you were reconciled, or "made peace," with someone.

3. What do you think is the root cause of anger?

4. Do you think there is "righteous anger"? How is that different from normal anger?

5. When we are angry, why do we often call people names, or label others? How effective is this?

6. Why do you think Jesus instructs people to deal with their anger quickly?

7. What would your advice be to someone who is angry with a friend or parent?

Live Like This:
One word that sums it up for you

5: Lust

Matthew 5:27-30

27*"You have heard the commandment that says, 'You must not commit adultery.' 28But I say, anyone who even looks at a woman with lust has already committed adultery with her in his heart. 29So if your eye—even your good eye—causes you to lust, gouge it out and throw it away. It is better for you to lose one part of your body than for your whole body to be thrown into hell. 30And if your hand—even your stronger hand—causes you to sin, cut it off and throw it away. It is better for you to lose one part of your body than for your whole body to be thrown into hell.*

Should a husband or wife break their marriage by having an affair? Of course not! Think of the wreckage that an affair has on a family. Jesus wants people to know that lust, or the desire to have what belongs to someone else, is a wrecking ball on the good life God wants for us.

The Bible is not against the beauty of a man or woman; God is the creator of beauty! God is not against love or sex; God made them both for our enjoyment. However, just as a fire belongs in a fireplace, there is a right place and time for these incredible gifts. A fire can cause incredible damage in the wrong place.

Jesus explains that there is a connection between our eyes and our heart. In summary, He says, "if you look... you have ... in your heart." The eyes are a gateway to our heart. What you put in front of your eyes is like a syringe injection straight into your heart. In the same way, we can avoid adultery and lust in our heart if we take control of our eyes. Job said, "I have made a covenant with my eyes not to look with lust at a young woman" (Job 31:1). Jesus' teaching on lust is applicable for women as well as men.

Later in this passage, Jesus teaches a principle about dealing with lust. If our eye causes us to lust, we don't have to literally gouge it out! Jesus is exaggerating intentionally to draw attention to the seriousness of lust. What Jesus means practically is "do not look". We need not cut off our hand, nor our feet, instead, if anything in our body causes us to lust, then don't use it. Act as if you don't have an eye, hand, or foot.

Jesus teaches that a lot is on the line when it comes to lust. Maybe you have seen in your own family or in a friend's family the kind of damage that lust or affairs can have. Lust can lead to hell on earth for those who have to deal with its impact. We must deliberately decline lust in our lives; it is one of the most powerful enemies of our faith. Meanwhile, we must remember that Jesus is on our team! Jesus offers forgiveness, restoration, and redemption for all who turn to Him.

1. On a scale of 1-10, how much sexual content is in our culture today? What are the consequences of this?

2. Have you seen the effect of an affair or broken relationship in a family you know? What has been the impact?

3. Why do you think God made beautiful things?

4. What would life be like if there were no beauty? Would it be better this way?

5. How much do you think a blind person would struggle with visual lust? What does this teach us about the use of our eyes?

6. What does our culture say about restraining ourselves from lust? Why?

7. Discuss any issues you may have personally with lust.

Live Like This:
One word that sums it up for you

6: Integrity

[31]*"You have heard the law that says, 'A man can divorce his wife by merely giving her a written notice of divorce.' [32]But I say that a man who divorces his wife, unless she has been unfaithful, causes her to commit adultery. And anyone who marries a divorced woman also commits adultery. [33]"You have also heard that our ancestors were told, 'You must not break your vows; you must carry out the vows you make to the LORD.' [34]But I say, do not make any vows! Do not say, 'By heaven!' because heaven is God's throne. [35]And do not say, 'By the earth!' because the earth is his footstool. And do not say, 'By Jerusalem!' for Jerusalem is the city of the great King. [36]Do not even say, 'By my head!' for you can't turn one hair white or black. [37]Just say a simple, 'Yes, I will,' or 'No, I won't.' Anything beyond this is from the evil one.*

What is possibly the most destructive event in a person's life summed up in one word? For some, the word is "divorce." Many of us we have experienced the pain and suffering of divorce in one way or another. A lot could be written here about divorce and what Jesus says about it. But rather than analyze divorce, let's take a look at a root issue of divorce: integrity.

Jesus' words in this section cover seven verses; two of the verses are about divorce and the other five verses discuss vows and promises. Jesus' emphasis on this topic is on becoming a person of integrity. Integrity means being "undivided," or in other words, to be a "person of your word."

Sometimes people try to convince others by saying things like "I swear on my mother's grave!" or "I swear on a stack of Bibles!" When the President of America is sworn into office, a hand is placed on a Bible as the Presidential oath is recited. Yet, Jesus tells us not to swear by anything, not heaven, not earth, not Jerusalem, nothing! We might ask ourselves, "why would Jesus not want me to add anything to my 'oath'?"

Jesus tells us to keep our promises simple. Jesus instructs us to say, "Yes, I will," or "No, I won't." Elsewhere in the Bible it states, "Just say a simple yes or no" (James 5:12). Giving a yes or no answer may sound simple enough, but it is incredibly hard to do consistently. In our society it is common to make excuses. It is also common to make promises that we never plan on keeping. Sometimes this even leads to divorce.

We can grow in integrity as we think carefully about each promise we make. Christians must work hard to keep their word, even when it is difficult (especially when it is difficult!) Christians should be the most trustworthy people on earth as they strive to be like Jesus. Meanwhile, when we fail, our Savior promises to continue to be with us.

1. Who is the most trustworthy person you know?

2. Why do you think divorce is such a painful experience?

3. Do you think "being a person of your word" has anything to do with marriage and divorce? Why or why not?

4. Why do you think people over thousands of years have tried to add phrases or extra sayings to their simple "yes" or "no?"

5. On a scale of 1-10, 10 being perfect, how trustworthy are you?

6. What is an example of a time when it was hard for you to keep a promise?

7. What would it say about Jesus if His followers were known for being incredibly reliable and trustworthy?

Live Like This:
One word that sums it up for you

7: Retaliation

Matthew 5:38-42

[38] *"You have heard that it was said, 'AN EYE FOR AN EYE, AND A TOOTH FOR A TOOTH.'* [39] *"But I say to you, do not resist an evil person; but whoever slaps you on your right cheek, turn the other to him also.* [40] *"If anyone wants to sue you and take your shirt, let him have your coat also.* [41] *"Whoever forces you to go one mile, go with him two.* [42] *"Give to him who asks of you, and do not turn away from him who wants to borrow from you."*

At first glance, this scripture might appear to be a lesson on how to be a "wimp." But after deeper reflection, it shows how to express an incredible measure of power – the same type of power that Jesus displayed while on earth.

In the Old Testament and ancient cultures, the saying "an eye for an eye" was common legal practice in a variety of cases. A problem arose when people started to act as their own court and judge. Jesus gives four different examples. It is important to know that they are examples of an underlying principle. The principle is the message. The examples are not the universal message for every situation, rather Jesus' focus is the principle, or the reason which undergirds, the application.

If we are slapped in the face, we are sharing in the experience of Jesus. While Jesus was on earth, He was slapped, hit, spit on, and mocked. However, Jesus did not retaliate, He simply held His ground (1 Peter 2:21-23). Immediate retaliation is the weakest response we can give.

Do not take the law into our own hands. If someone does something illegal, alert the authorities! God is the Christian's ultimate authority, He is the one who will judge and make everything right. When we are offended, or hurt, we know that everything will eventually be made right in a way that is more powerful than anything we can do at that moment. The true Authority has already been alerted!

No one may have modeled Jesus' ethic on retaliation better than Martin Luther King Jr., who based his civil-rights movement on this scripture. His house was bombed, he faced death threats every day for thirteen years, he was accused of being Communist, he was stabbed by a member of his own race, he was jailed over twenty times, and he was shot to death. Yet he said, "hate multiplies hate." He also said, "love is the only force capable of transforming an enemy into a friend," and "meet hate with love." His actions spoke louder than his words in the face of evil. Those who want to live like Jesus can show it by their actions in the face of evil.

1. What is your gut reaction when someone hurts you?

2. Is it weak or wimpy to not retaliate? Why or why not?

3. What is the general principle behind this scripture?

4. What can we learn from Martin Luther King Jr. regarding Christian retaliation?

5. What should you do if...

    A. Someone makes fun of your faith?

    B. Someone punches you in the face?

    C. Someone hurts your friend?

Live Like This:
One word that sums it up for you

8: Love

Matthew 5:43-48

[43]*"You have heard that it was said, 'Love your neighbor and hate your enemy.'* [44]*But I tell you: Love your enemies and pray for those who persecute you,* [45]*that you may be sons of your Father in heaven. He causes his sun to rise on the evil and the good, and sends rain on the righteous and the unrighteous.* [46]*If you love those who love you, what reward will you get? Are not even the tax collectors doing that?* [47]*And if you greet only your brothers, what are you doing more than others? Do not even pagans do that?* [48]*Be perfect, therefore, as your heavenly Father is perfect.*

It is natural for us to treat our friends better than our enemies. Yet, Jesus challenges those who call themselves Christians to stand out in a strange way. In Jesus' time the religious teachers added endless details to God's commands. We are to love our neighbor, it says so directly in Leviticus 19:18, but nowhere does scripture tell us to hate our enemies. In reality, scripture tells us, "If your enemies are hungry, give them food to eat. If they are thirsty, give them water to drink" (Proverbs 25:21).

Christians are commanded to love their enemies. Jesus tells us to pray for our enemies. In Luke 6:27, Jesus tells us to bless our enemies and do good to them. Pray, bless, and do good to our enemies. But why?

In verse 45, we see that God lets the sun rise on good and evil people. God also sends rain on both of them. So why should we treat "evil" enemies with love? Because God does too. We are to be like our Father in heaven, literally children of our Father, so we need to act like our Father. Loving all people is what our "family" should be about (see verse 45).

For those who stand against us, we are called to do not the ordinary, but the extraordinary, just as Jesus Christ was willing to die for the worst of us. People should be able to notice that Christians are different. One way to show that Christians are different is in the way we treat our enemies; in the way we treat "evil" people.

No one can be perfect in this life. 1 John 1:8 says that, "If we claim we have no sin, we are only fooling ourselves and not living in the truth." But this doesn't mean that we can go around hating people we don't like or even those who have hurt us. We are to take our aim on being "perfect" and nothing less, while accepting the love and forgiveness that God gives us each step of the way. It is only our faith and daily trust in Jesus that can help us to live like Jesus.

1. Who is your "neighbor"?

Name a neighbor (past or present):_____

2. Who is your "enemy"?

Name an enemy (past or present):_____

3. Have you ever hated anyone? Why?

4. Why are Christians instructed to love our "enemies"?

5. Explain some specific ways you could pray, bless, or do good for an enemy.

6. How can we muster up the courage to change the way we treat our enemies?

7. Do you think we can become "perfect"? If not, should we not even try?

Live Like This:
One word that sums it up for you

9: Giving

Matthew 6:1-4

[1]"Watch out! Don't do your good deeds publicly, to be admired by others, for you will lose the reward from your Father in heaven. [2]When you give to someone in need, don't do as the hypocrites do—blowing trumpets in the synagogues and streets to call attention to their acts of charity! I tell you the truth, they have received all the reward they will ever get. [3]But when you give to someone in need, don't let your left hand know what your right hand is doing. [4]Give your gifts in private, and your Father, who sees everything, will reward you.

In the previous lessons and verses, Jesus taught mostly about internal things like love and integrity. Now, Jesus turns His teachings to a few external topics. In this section of scripture, Jesus teaches about good deeds and giving, which are outward actions. Yet, Jesus is still concerned with what happens on the inside of a person. Our internal and external life are always connected. Christians and those who are not Christians both do good deeds and give to others, but Jesus is telling His followers to do these in a unique way.

First, Jesus starts with a warning: "Watch out!" If the God of the universe says "Watch out", we'd better pay attention to this warning. Jesus' warning is against doing good deeds for personal publicity or to be admired. If we do this, we will lose our true reward.

Jesus turns His attention to a particular good deed: the act of giving. Notice that Jesus doesn't say, "if" you give, but "when" you give. Christians are expected to be people who give away their time, possessions, and talents to help others. When we give, we don't need to "toot our own horn" or draw attention to ourselves. If the reward that we seek is publicity and fame, then we have accomplished that and have no further reward. If we avoid self-promotion, there is a greater reward in store.

Earlier, in Matthew 5:16, we were told to "let our good deeds shine out for all to see." Do Jesus' words in this section contradict His earlier words? The key is our motivation. We should show our deeds when we are tempted to hide them, and hide our deeds when tempted to show them. There is a right time for each.

When we give, we should not let our left hand know what our right hand is doing. Do not promote your actions publicly (unless you actually want to hide them). Do not give to make ourselves just feel better on the inside. So why should we give? Because Jesus tell us to, and we want to please Him. Our true reward will be in filling the need and honoring God.

1. Describe someone famous who "self-promotes". How does this make you feel?

2. List 10 reasons why people do good deeds or give money.

1.   6.
2.   7.
3.   8.
4.   9.
5.   10.

3. Describe a time when someone gave you something meaningful. How did it make you feel?

4. How would you feel if someone did something for you just so everyone would know what they did?

5. When is it right to "let our good deeds shine?" When is right to hide them?

6. What are some ways you could give of your time, possessions, or talents to people who need them?

8. What is a way that you could do this that would honor God?

Live Like This:
One word that sums it up for you

10: Prayer (Part 1)

Matthew 6:5-8

[5]*"When you pray, don't be like the hypocrites who love to pray publicly on street corners and in the synagogues where everyone can see them. I tell you the truth, that is all the reward they will ever get.* [6]*But when you pray, go away by yourself, shut the door behind you, and pray to your Father in private. Then your Father, who sees everything, will reward you.* [7]*"When you pray, don't babble on and on as people of other religions do. They think their prayers are answered merely by repeating their words again and again.* [8]*Don't be like them, for your Father knows exactly what you need even before you ask him!*

If we want to live like Jesus, then we need to know what He says about prayer. Jesus begins His discussion about prayer by identifying "when" you pray. Like the previous section about giving, Jesus expects us to pray; not "if" we pray, but "when" we pray.

When we pray, we must not be like hypocrites. In Jesus' day, a hypocrite was technically an actor in a play. The actor would pretend to be someone else. Jesus is criticizing those who were pretending to be people who were praying for the right reasons, but in reality, prayed just to get attention (i.e. "look at me!" / "listen to me!").

Jesus gives two practical suggestions for prayer. First, Jesus tells us to pray in private. We can go into our room, close the door, and be alone while we pray. Why should we do this? It will help us focus on the real aim of prayer: communication with God. Prayer is not primarily others who might be around to hear it. Prayer is talking directly with God.

The second suggestion Jesus gives for prayer is for prayer to be brief. There is no benefit to mindlessly saying the same words over and over. In normal conversations no one would say the same thing over and over. No one says, "Today is a beautiful day. Today is a beautiful day. Today is a beautiful day [over and over]". So it is with God. Jesus wants our minds to be engaged, not just our lips.

So, is it wrong to pray with other people or even to repeat anything? No. Christian prayer is generally brief and to the point. Jesus prayed in the garden of Gethsemane and at various times for a very long time. As you can see, a strict formula is not what Jesus has in mind. Rigid religion is what the Pharisee's had in mind. Jesus has *recommendations*, not rigid rules, that will help our personal relationship grow close to God because Jesus wants us to talk him simply and naturally.

1. Why do you think people pray?

2. When was a memorable time when you or someone else prayed?

3. Hypocrites in Jesus' time prayed just to be noticed by people. Does this still happen?

4. Why do you think Jesus recommends praying alone? Is there a time when praying with others is also helpful?

5. What do you think are the benefits of prayer?

6. How do you feel about praying? Has this changed over time?

7. If prayer is a conversation, how to you think God can talk back to us?

Live Like This:
One word that sums it up for you

11: Prayer (Part 2)

Matthew 6:9-13

⁹Pray like this: Our Father in heaven, may your name be kept holy. ¹⁰May your Kingdom come soon. May your will be done on earth, as it is in heaven. ¹¹Give us today the food we need, ¹²and forgive us our sins, as we have forgiven those who sin against us. ¹³And don't let us yield to temptation, but rescue us from the evil one.

Jesus has a lot to say about prayer. In the verses that precede this section, Jesus gives some practical *instructions* about prayer and our reasons for praying. In this section, Jesus gives us an incredible *example* prayer.

When we pray, we are told to, "Ask, using my name, and you will receive, and you will have abundant joy." (John 16:24) One way to look at this prayer, commonly called "The Lord's Prayer," is to think of it as Jesus saying, "talk to me like this."

The Lord's prayer can be separated in two sections. The first section declares *facts* about God. God is 1) Our Father, 2) In Heaven, and 3) Holy. When we pray, we are praying to someone who is entirely beyond us. God is perfect, God is in heaven, and we are so unlike Him in so many ways. Yet, the first description is that God is our Father. We are His children; God is literally our Father. This is such a great reminder for those of us who have struggled with our relationship with our parents, or anyone who has a low self-image. We are children of the King of the Universe. Prayer is like talking to an unbelievable parent with unending resources.

The first section continues to focus on who God is and His purposes. Before we ask anything *of* God, we should commit ourselves to trust God's will and purposes for His Kingdom. Prayer is not to build *our* Kingdom, or *our* plans, or *our* wishes, but God's Kingdom and God's plans. Prayer can help bring heaven down to earth in our hearts and in our daily world.

The second section of the Lord's prayer has to do with our needs. Jesus reminds us of several types of needs: 1) Our physical needs like food, 2) Our spiritual needs like forgiveness from God, 3) Our relational needs like forgiving our friends, and 4) Lastly, our need for help from temptation.

This prayer of Jesus is incredible and worthwhile to memorize and say often. Although just two verses before (Matthew 6:7), Jesus tells us that prayer is not about repeating words over and over, this prayer is a great guide for genuine, original, and heartfelt prayer. Take a moment to pray it right now.

1. Have you ever heard The Lord's Prayer before? If so, when and where?

2. List at least 10 reasons or situations for which people pray:

1)   6)
2)   7)
3)   8)
4)   9)
5)   10)

3. The first part of this prayer takes time to declare facts about God. Why do you think this is important?

4. Why do you think this prayer reminds us that God is holy and in heaven?

5. Why do you think this prayer reminds us that God is our Father? What does that mean to you?

6. List some needs you have that you could bring to God in prayer:

1) Physical needs
2) Spiritual needs
3) Relationship needs
4) Help in temptation

Live Like This:
One word that sums it up for you

12: Forgiveness

Matthew 6:14-15

[14] *"If you forgive those who sin against you, your heavenly Father will forgive you.* [15] *But if you refuse to forgive others, your Father will not forgive your sins.*

In the previous prayer, in Matthew 6:9-13, we are told to pray, "forgive us our sins as we have forgiven those who sin against us." Jesus adds something surprising following this prayer. There are a couple questions that need to be addressed. First, what does it mean to forgive? Second, what does it mean that the Father may not forgive me? Third, what should I do if I am having a hard time forgiving someone?

What does it mean to forgive? Forgiving is so much more than simply saying "sorry." When you say "sorry" you are simply saying how you feel without really understanding how the other person feels about the situation. It is a "one-way" transaction that focuses mostly on making yourself feel better. True forgiveness is a two-way exchange. True forgiveness forces us to enter into community. When you say, "will you forgive me?", a response is required. This question provides the opportunity for both people to come to peace.

Does this scripture mean that God will not forgive me if I can't forgive others? Yes, and no. We are saved by grace, not by works, as Ephesians 2:8-9 says, "God saved you by his grace when you believed. And you can't take credit for this; it is a gift from God. Salvation is not a reward for the good things we have done, so none of us can boast about it." So our salvation is not in question. Salvation is a gift, not a reward. What is in trouble is our relationship with God, not our salvation. If you are having a hard time with your parents, you are still their child. Yet, your relationship is hurt by this problem. So our salvation is not in jeopardy, but our relationship with God is severely hurt when we will not forgive others (not to mention our relationship with those we will not forgive).

If you are having a hard time forgiving someone, you are not alone. Forgiveness can be difficult - sometimes very difficult. Pray and ask God for His heart. God knows a lot about forgiving others. Stop and think about your own mistakes and how God has forgiven you. When you are ready to forgive, go to the person directly and don't make excuses. Don't use the words "but", "if", or "maybe." Admit your fault specifically, in detail, and how it may have hurt the other person. You may have to accept the consequences and change your behavior. Not only will you find peace with the person and great sense of relief, but you will find greater peace with God.

1. What gets more attention, when people make mistakes or when they correct their mistakes? Why?

2. Describe a time when someone asked you to forgive them.

3. Describe a time when you asked someone for forgiveness.

4. Why do you think God forgives you?

5. Which group of people is easiest to forgive? Which is hardest? Why?

Stranger | New Friend | Casual Friend |Close Friend | Sibling | Parents

6. What advice would you give to a friend who was having a hard time forgiving someone? Think through various situations.

7. Is there anyone you need ask to forgive you? Why?

Live Like This:
One word that sums it up for you

13: Fasting

Matthew 6:16-19

[16]*"And when you fast, don't make it obvious, as the hypocrites do, for they try to look miserable and disheveled so people will admire them for their fasting. I tell you the truth, that is the only reward they will ever get.* [17]*But when you fast, comb your hair and wash your face.* [18]*Then no one will notice that you are fasting, except your Father, who knows what you do in private. And your Father, who sees everything, will reward you.* [19]*"Don't store up treasures here on earth, where moths eat them and rust destroys them, and where thieves break in and steal.*

First off, let's clear something up... Fasting has nothing to do with speed. In fact, fasting actually helps us slow down. Wouldn't it be nice to slow down a little? Let me explain. Fasting is to *not* do something. Fasting means to abstain from something or an activity. Traditionally, to fast means to not eat food. In fact, the English word "breakfast" means to "break our fast" from not eating while we sleep. In other words, in the morning the last time we ate was the day before, then we took a break from eating, went to sleep, and we "break our fast" and eat in the morning.

Of the three primary activities Jesus encourages in the Sermon on the Mount (which are praying, giving and fasting), fasting is the activity that is the least familiar to most. Praying is similar to talking. Giving is something people do at birthdays and other events. But, fasting is something that might be totally new to most people; there are not many parallels to fasting in our society. Dieting or skipping meals to lose weight is completely different from fasting. Biblical fasting is about an internal change, as opposed to the worldly approach which aims at an external change.

The easiest way to think about fasting is to purposely stop doing something you are used to doing in order to remind you of your dependence on God. If you skip a meal, use that time to focus on God. If you give up watching TV for a night, use that time to read your Bible or listen to some worship music. The idea is to replace something with something else. We are creatures of habit, so when we skip a meal, our mind and stomach remind us almost every minute or two, "you normally eat right now, what are you doing?!" Then, you answer your stomach by saying, "the reason I'm not eating is that I'm feeding my soul instead of my stomach." Take that, stomach.

We learn from this section of scripture that when we fast, we should not draw attention to ourselves; fasting is mostly a private thing. Any investment in your spiritual life will benefit you more than any wealth here on earth because your spiritual investment lasts forever.

1. What have you tried to stop doing temporarily for a specific purpose?

2. What is your gut reaction to the idea of fasting?

3. What would be the hardest activity for you to stop temporarily? Why?

Eating	Internet	Junk Food
Snacking	Video Games	Soda or Coffee
TV	Sports	Spending Money

4. Why do you think Jesus recommends fasting to help you grow spiritually?

5. What kinds of investments are you making in your spiritual life right now?

6. What is a struggle or challenge in your life that you would like to see change? Do you think fasting from one thing or another could help you draw on God's power to see that change? Would you consider fasting for this reason this week? If so, write out your plan.

Live Like This:
One word that sums it up for you

14: Heart

Matthew 6:19-24

¹⁹*"Don't store up treasures here on earth, where moths eat them and rust destroys them, and where thieves break in and steal.* ²⁰*Store your treasures in heaven, where moths and rust cannot destroy, and thieves do not break in and steal.* ²¹*Wherever your treasure is, there the desires of your heart will also be.* ²²*"Your eye is a lamp that provides light for your body. When your eye is good, your whole body is filled with light.* ²³*But when your eye is bad, your whole body is filled with darkness. And if the light you think you have is actually darkness, how deep that darkness is!* ²⁴*"No one can serve two masters. For you will hate one and love the other; you will be devoted to one and despise the other. You cannot serve both God and money.*

In the previous sections of scripture, Jesus focused on *private* actions for His followers such as prayer, giving and fasting. Now, in this section, Jesus turns His attention to some of the *public* actions of someone who wants to live like Jesus. Jesus opens His discussion of public actions by teaching us about our heart.

Jesus begins by addressing the treasures of our heart. He contrasts the types of treasures that last with things that don't last very long. In Jesus' day, people would store their valuables, such as precious metals and expensive clothes, but these were always susceptible to rusting or being eaten by moths. Imagine going to grab your most valuable piece of jewelry and it has literally rusted into flakes of metallic dust! Jesus teaches us to invest in treasure in heaven, which is anything on earth whose effects last for eternity.

Next, Jesus teaches about the eyes of our heart. Our eyes can be thought of as the door of our heart and mind. Our eyes literally let light into our body and mind. We choose what we let into our heart and our mind as we choose what we look at with our eyes. We can choose to look at wonderful godly things to fill us with God's light, or we can choose to look at things that will bring darkness into our heart. The choice is ours.

The last heart-challenge is to examine the devotion of our hearts. Jesus says we cannot be devoted to two things at the same time. We are designed to have a one-track mind and heart. Jesus shows us that, often, our devotion is to money above all else. The distractions of our hearts are different for everyone, but to live like Jesus we need to be singled-hearted in our devotion to God.

In order to properly attend to the *public* actions Jesus wants us to do, we must first pay close attention to our hearts.

1. Name 10 popular "treasures" your friends want:

1.   6.
2.   7.
3.   8.
4.   9.
5.   10.

2. How would you define a person's "heart"?

3. Since your eyes enlighten your heart, what would your heart look like after what you have looked at today?

4. What do you think other people would say you are devoted to?

5. If treasure in heaven is anything on earth whose effects last for eternity, give some examples of treasures in heaven.

6. If you were to be remembered at your funeral for one thing, what would you like that to be?

7. How can someone change their heart based on this section of scripture?

Live Like This:
One word that sums it up for you

15: Worry

Matthew 6:25-34

25"That is why I tell you not to worry about everyday life—whether you have enough food and drink, or enough clothes to wear. Isn't life more than food, and your body more than clothing? 26Look at the birds. They don't plant or harvest or store food in barns, for your heavenly Father feeds them. And aren't you far more valuable to him than they are? 27Can all your worries add a single moment to your life? 28"And why worry about your clothing? Look at the lilies of the field and how they grow. They don't work or make their clothing, 29yet Solomon in all his glory was not dressed as beautifully as they are. 30And if God cares so wonderfully for wildflowers that are here today and thrown into the fire tomorrow, he will certainly care for you. Why do you have so little faith? 31"So don't worry about these things, saying, 'What will we eat? What will we drink? What will we wear?' 32These things dominate the thoughts of unbelievers, but your heavenly Father already knows all your needs. 33Seek the Kingdom of God above all else, and live righteously, and he will give you everything you need. 34"So don't worry about tomorrow, for tomorrow will bring its own worries. Today's trouble is enough for today.

Jesus said that we can't serve both God and money. Even if we don't *serve* money, we can be tempted to *worry* about it nonstop! To live like Jesus, we must counter our worry with faith in God.

Even though the Sermon on the Mount was written two thousand years ago, Jesus knew that we would worry. Worry is not a modern invention; it has been around forever. Worry is a temptation based in a lack of trust. If God provides for the birds and the lilies, why would He not provide for us? In many ways, worry is the opposite of faith.

If we are commanded not to worry, can we sit around and be lazy? No. We need something on which to set our minds, our hearts, our ambition, and our inner motivation. If our ambition is for *my* future, *my* clothing, *my* home, *my* food, *my* career... then we do have something to be concerned about, we have plenty to worry about. If we are looking for *God's* future for our life, *God's* promise to clothe and feed us, *God's* ideal place for us to live, *God's* career for us... then we are in a place of faith and have no need to worry.

Jesus gives us great advice when we worry: Seek God first. Transfer our worry to ambition for God's kingdom and His righteousness, and then we have no need to worry about anything.

1. On a scale of 1-10, how much do you worry? Why?

2. What are some things that your friends and family worry about?

3. Why do you think that Jesus talks about birds and flowers when talking about worry?

4. What does worry have to do with faith?

5. How does worry affect you personally?

6. What does this scripture say how to get "everything you need?"

7. What is something you are tempted to worry about right now? How do you think you should respond after this study?

Live Like This:
One word that sums it up for you

16: Judging

Matthew 7:1-6

¹"Do not judge others, and you will not be judged. ²For you will be treated as you treat others. The standard you use in judging is the standard by which you will be judged. ³"And why worry about a speck in your friend's eye when you have a log in your own? ⁴How can you think of saying to your friend, 'Let me help you get rid of that speck in your eye,' when you can't see past the log in your own eye? ⁵Hypocrite! First get rid of the log in your own eye; then you will see well enough to deal with the speck in your friend's eye. ⁶"Don't waste what is holy on people who are unholy. Don't throw your pearls to pigs! They will trample the pearls, then turn and attack you.

Are you perfect? No one is. Jesus doesn't expect people to be perfect. When we see others misbehaving around us, how should we respond? Should we ignore it? Should we correct it? Simply put, Jesus teaches us that we must not judge others.

What does it mean to "judge?" It does not mean that it is wrong to have lawyers, policemen, or simply ignore things that are wrong. To obey Jesus' instructions on judging does not mean that we have to lie and agree that 2+2=5. What Jesus condemns is when we try to read into the motivations behind a wrongful action. Judging is when we assume we know the heart or motive behind an action. Judging means that we try to understand all the reasons something has happened. Judging is basically when we try to play "god." When people say, "you can't judge me," we *can* evaluate their actions, but we *cannot* evaluate their hearts. Heart-judgement is God's business.

To live like Jesus, we need to follow His instructions. Jesus tells us to remove the "log" in our own eye before we remove the "speck" in our brother's eye. It is easy to recognize failures in other people and hard to notice our own. Jesus' teaching doesn't tell us to forget our friend's failures, but to deal with them after we have first dealt with ourselves. When we ignore a problem or conflict we recognize, it robs us of an opportunity to be refined in our faith and also robs our friends of that opportunity, too.

There is a time and a place to help people. When someone is so far out of control that they reject anyone and anything related to God, we should consider Jesus' word to find the right place and time to talk to them. This might take some patience.

We have an incredible opportunity to help our friends in their challenges, but we must be careful to examine ourselves and our motives.

1. If you were to give yourself a grade (ex: A+, C-, F), what would you give yourself for "judging others?" Why?

2. Have you ever heard someone say, "Don't judge me," or "You can't judge me"? What do you think they mean by that?

3. What is the difference between judging an action and a motive? Why does Jesus warn us to not judge motives?

4. Give an example of a situation where you have seen the "speck" in someone else while ignoring the "log" in yourself.

5. Explain the process Jesus teaches us from these scriptures of what we should do when we see something wrong in another person.

6. How does "timing" play a role in correcting or confronting another person?

7. Why are we tempted to judge people the wrong way?

Live Like This:
One word that sums it up for you

17: Prayer (Part 3)

Matthew 7:7-12

7"Keep on asking, and you will receive what you ask for. Keep on seeking, and you will find. Keep on knocking, and the door will be opened to you. 8For everyone who asks, receives. Everyone who seeks, finds. And to everyone who knocks, the door will be opened. 9"You parents—if your children ask for a loaf of bread, do you give them a stone instead? 10Or if they ask for a fish, do you give them a snake? Of course not! 11So if you sinful people know how to give good gifts to your children, how much more will your heavenly Father give good gifts to those who ask him. 12"Do to others whatever you would like them to do to you. This is the essence of all that is taught in the law and the prophets.

Some people approach prayer as God's vending machine. They think, "I push the button for what I want and then I wait for it to drop in my hand." There is much more to prayer than that. Vending machine prayer not only makes ourselves our own god in a sense, but it also would be unwise to always get what we want. In this scripture, Jesus gives us insight into our attitude in prayer.

Jesus tells us to ask, seek, and knock in our prayers. Jesus teaches us to be persistent in prayer. Jesus says to *keep on* asking, *keep on* seeking, *keep on* knocking. We are to always be persistent in our prayers. One thing that we miss in the English grammar is that the verb is plural: keep on asking together, keep on seeking *together*, keep on knocking *together*. We can pray alone, but we should also pray with others.

If we ask, seek and knock, shouldn't we also receive, find, and see open doors? The answer is: yes! But, sometimes the door that opens has something behind it that is unexpected. Anyone who has ever prayed knows that you don't always get what you want. Jesus teaches us this when He says (in verse 11) that the heavenly Father gives *good* gifts to those who ask him. God will only give us what is good for us, and only God ultimately knows what is truly good for us. If you don't get what you prayed for, then something better is in store, for our heavenly Father will give us what is better.

With this in mind, it is of ultimate importance that we search the Bible thoroughly to know more about God's will for our life so that we will be able to know, trust and desire what is best (from God's point of view).

This scripture ends with the "golden rule." It is fitting that even God does unto others what He would want done for Himself, which is whatever will do the most good. We can model God's heart as we treat others in a godly way and as we try to do the most good for them that we can.

1. What is something that you have been very persistent about?

2. On a scale of 1-10 (1 low, 10 high), how much do you think people expect answers to their prayers. Why?

3. Do you have any examples of answered prayer in your life? Describe.

4. Verse 11 says that the heavenly Father only gives good gifts. Do you think that He ever gives bad gifts, or bad answers to prayer?

5. Who is someone you know that tends obey the "golden rule?"

6. Is the "golden rule" selfish? Why or why not?

7. What is something that you want to pray about persistently?

Live Like This:
One word that sums it up for you

18: Loneliness

Matthew 7:13-14

[13] *"You can enter God's Kingdom only through the narrow gate. The highway to hell is broad, and its gate is wide for the many who choose that way.* [14] *But the gateway to life is very narrow and the road is difficult, and only a few ever find it.*

The road to Jesus is the "gateway to life!" But, the road to Jesus is also difficult. This scripture begins by discussing how to enter God's kingdom. Once we enter God's kingdom, it is a one-way road, or a gate that only swings in one direction. We cannot go back and forth between narrow and wide roads. We all start on the wide road and some will enter the narrow road, but not many.

The highway to hell is broad. It has been said that anyone can destroy a lifetime of hard work with 15 minutes of bad decisions. It is easy to go down that road because it is the one we would choose on our own if God did not exist. The broad road is a road filled with short-lived hype that gets us excited like a sugar-rush but then drops us down and we end up more tired than before. Many choose the broad road.

The road to true and full life is difficult and challenging. It is one that we do not choose on our own. It is narrow, difficult, and as Jesus puts it, "only a few ever find it." Because of this, anyone on this road can feel lonely. While we are alive on this earth, those on the wide road have full view of those on the narrow road. Yet, the roads lead in very different directions.

When a person begins a relationship with Jesus it often is accompanied with hugs, congratulations, and people who affirm this decision. But, this initial moment ends and soon it becomes obvious that there are many more people on the wide road than on the narrow road. The wide road looks appealing from a distance and there are more people there. This leads many to question their relationship with God and to feel a sense of loneliness. But, the narrow road does offer something the wide road cannot: a relationship with Jesus Christ and hope for the future!

Later in the gospel of Matthew, Jesus says, "Take my yoke upon you. Let me teach you, because I am humble and gentle at heart, and you will find rest for your souls. For my yoke is easy to bear, and the burden I give you is light." (Matthew 11:29-30) The narrow road offers a companion: Jesus Himself. The wide road offers no companion. Just ask anyone who has been on the wide road for a while, it is the true path of loneliness. The narrow road, however, offers an eternal companion.

1. Explain any "roads" in your life that have been different from your family or friends.

2. How would you describe the "wide road" Jesus talks about?

3. How would you describe the "narrow road" Jesus talks about?

4. Have you ever experienced loneliness because of Jesus? If so, how?

5. Do you think people on the "wide road" experience loneliness? If so, explain.

6. In Matthew 11:29-30, Jesus says that His yoke, or the direction He helps us go, is easy and the burden is light. How can this be if it says in Matthew 7:13-14 that the narrow road is difficult?

7. How can a personal relationship with Jesus affect us when we are lonely?

Live Like This:
One word that sums it up for you

19: Fruitfulness

Matthew 7:15-23

¹⁵*"Beware of false prophets who come disguised as harmless sheep but are really vicious wolves. ¹⁶You can identify them by their fruit, that is, by the way they act. Can you pick grapes from thornbushes, or figs from thistles? ¹⁷A good tree produces good fruit, and a bad tree produces bad fruit. ¹⁸A good tree can't produce bad fruit, and a bad tree can't produce good fruit. ¹⁹So every tree that does not produce good fruit is chopped down and thrown into the fire. ²⁰Yes, just as you can identify a tree by its fruit, so you can identify people by their actions. ²¹"Not everyone who calls out to me, 'Lord! Lord!' will enter the Kingdom of Heaven. Only those who actually do the will of my Father in heaven will enter. ²²On judgment day many will say to me, 'Lord! Lord! We prophesied in your name and cast out demons in your name and performed many miracles in your name.' ²³But I will reply, 'I never knew you. Get away from me, you who break God's laws.'*

"Beware" is how Jesus begins this section. If Jesus says "beware," we must pay close attention to what He is about to say. We must beware because the threats, as Jesus says, are "disguised."

We need to beware of the false promises of the world. These can come to us through "false prophets." These false prophets give us visions and dreams from their own minds and their own desires, not God's. These are false hopes that never live up to their promise. Often times, the false promises of the world are the objects and experiences that claim they will give us peace and happiness but always leave us wanting more.

We need to beware of fake fruit. Sometimes people or activities can look like they are good for us, but in reality, they lead us in the wrong direction. The best way to tell is to look at the "fruit" they are producing. Just like an apple tree is supposed to produce apples, a relationship with God is supposed to produce love, joy, peace, patience, kindness, goodness, faithfulness, gentleness, and self-control (Galatians 5:22-23). If someone claims to be connected to Jesus, over time, this is the type of person they will become.

We need to beware of people who talk-the-talk, but don't walk-the-walk. Not everyone who says "Lord! Lord!" are true followers of Jesus, only those who actually do the will of God, those who walk-the-walk. A relationship with Jesus requires not mere verbal agreement, or even enthusiastic agreement of faith in Christ, but obedience in day-to-day life.

There are a lot of things to beware; the key is to know God in a personal and dependent way. If we know God and seek to obey him, we will be fruitful.

1. Where do you see signs that say "beware"? (For example: on a bottle of poison.)

2. What are situations in which people actually wear disguises in real life? What are typically the motives of these people?

3. How can you tell if someone is being shifty or deceptive? Give a personal example.

4. What are the "fruits" or byproducts of a true follower of Jesus?

5. How does it make you feel when you see Christians "talk-the-talk but not walk-the-walk?"

6. Why do you think Jesus discredits those who only say "Lord! Lord!"?

7. What kind of spiritual fruit would you like to see in your life?

Live Like This:
One word that sums it up for you

20: Review

Matthew 7:24-29

24"Anyone who listens to my teaching and follows it is wise, like a person who builds a house on solid rock. 25Though the rain comes in torrents and the floodwaters rise and the winds beat against that house, it won't collapse because it is built on bedrock. 26But anyone who hears my teaching and doesn't obey it is foolish, like a person who builds a house on sand. 27When the rains and floods come and the winds beat against that house, it will collapse with a mighty crash." 28When Jesus had finished saying these things, the crowds were amazed at his teaching, 29for he taught with real authority— quite unlike their teachers of religious law."

Have you been listening? Hopefully! What is even more important is if you are following in Jesus' footsteps. Listening and following are two very different things. Listening is a great start. Jesus spoke the Sermon on the Mount to a crowd of people. What we don't know is who decided to follow its challenges.

Jesus gives some examples of how we can know who is just listening and who is following in His steps. These examples talk about rain, floods, and wind; what Jesus is really doing is using a metaphor about the challenges we all face in our lives. These challenges could be our family, school, work, personal life, or a number of other things. In these challenges, our foundation is often revealed. Have we been simply listeners, or followers of Jesus? Often, a genuine follower of Jesus and a mere listener will look alike; they can both *hear* the same thing, but it often takes a storm to reveal the truth.

As Jesus concludes the Sermon on the Mount, the crowds were amazed (which can also mean they were astonished and even shocked.) If you can read the Sermon on the Mount and, at the end, feel the same as before having read it, then you missed it. Reread through it slower. Think how you can put it into practice. The Sermon on the Mount is a manual on how to be "counter-culture." Its message is against the flow of our society!

The last idea of the Sermon on the Mount is that Jesus taught unlike any other teacher they had ever heard. Jesus had authority; He was literally authoring the way to live right before their eyes. He told them: Live like this...

If you have sensed Jesus' authority and power in your life, then the Sermon on the Mount will resonate with your new heart and new life in Christ. Deep down, not only will you want to live like Jesus, but over time you will see Jesus Christ change your life through His power.

1. Have you ever listened to someone talk and realized that you don't remember anything they said? Why do you think this happens?

2. Is there a topic you know a lot about, but you don't actually put into action? Describe.

3. What are some of the "storms" and challenges that you have gone through?

4. How can a "storm" show a person's priorities and foundation in life?

5. If you were to go through a difficult challenge in your life, what do you think would show through? What would others hopefully notice in your life?

6. How can you build the foundation of your life deeper in Jesus Christ?

7. As you think back through the challenges Jesus presents in the Sermon on the Mount, do any shock or amaze you? If so, describe these.

Live Like This:
One word that sums it up for you

Notes